CIVIC VALUES

PROPERTY
RIGHTS

KAITLIN SCIRRI

Cavendish
Square
New York

Published in 2018 by Cavendish Square Publishing, LLC
243 5th Avenue, Suite 136, New York, NY 10016

First Edition

Website: cavendishsq.com

This publication represents the opinions and views of the author based on his or her personal experience, knowledge, and research. The information in this book serves as a general guide only. The author and publisher have used their best efforts in preparing this book and disclaim liability rising directly or indirectly from the use and application of this book.

All websites were available and accurate when this book was sent to press.

Library of Congress Cataloging-in-Publication Data

Names: Scirri, Kaitlin, author.
Title: Property rights / Kaitlin Scirri.
Description: New York : Cavendish Square Publishing, 2018. | Series: Civic values | Includes index.
Identifiers: LCCN 2017020194 (print) | LCCN 2017020463 (ebook) |
ISBN 9781502632036 (E-book) | ISBN 9781502632005 (pbk.) |
ISBN 9781502632029 (library bound) | ISBN 9781502632012 (6 pack)
Subjects: LCSH: Right of property--United States.
Classification: LCC KF562 (ebook) | LCC KF562 .S43 2018 (print) | DDC 346.7304/2--dc23
LC record available at https://lccn.loc.gov/2017020194

Editorial Director: David McNamara
Editor: Kristen Susienka
Copy Editor: Rebecca Rohan
Associate Art Director: Amy Greenan
Designer: Alan Sliwinski
Production Coordinator: Karol Szymczuk
Photo Research: J8 Media

The photographs in this book are used by permission and through the courtesy of: Front cover, Sean Locke Photography/Shutterstock.com; Back cover and throughout the book, Arosoft/Shutterstock.com; p. 4 Arina P. Habich/Shutterstock.com; p. 8 George Rinhart/Corbis/Getty Images; p. 9 Kevin Dodge/Corbis/Getty Images; p. 10 DEA/A. Dagli Orti/De Agostini Picture Library/Getty Images; p. 13 Orange Line Media/Shutterstock.com; p. 14 Aaron Haupt /Science Source/Getty Images; p. 16 Charles Édouard Armand-Dumaresq (1826-1895)/The White House Historical Association (White House Collection)/File: Signing of Declaration of Independence by Armand-Dumaresq, c1873 - restored.jpg/Wikimedia Commons; p. 18 Derivative work: Frank Schulenburg (talk)/File: Declaration of Independence draft (detail with changes by Franklin).jpg/Wikimedia Commons; p. 19 Tyler Olson/Shutterstock.com; p. 20 Vstock/Getty Images; p. 21 Kelly vanDellen/Shutterstock.com; p. 22 Africa Studio/Shutterstock.com; p. 24 Syda Productions/Shutterstock.com; p. 26 Monkey Business Images/Shutterstock.com; p. 27 Cynthia Farmer/Shutterstock.com; p. 28 Andy Dean Photography/Shutterstock.com.

Printed in the United States of America

CONTENTS

A neighborhood is made up of private homes and community property.

CHAPTER ONE

WHAT ABOUT PROPERTY RIGHTS?

Civic values play an important part of everyday living. What are they, though? They are ways people can work together to make a community fun and safe. Some examples are respecting others, listening to others, accepting everyone, and taking care of each other's property.

Property rights are important civic values. They are laws that allow citizens to own land, buildings, and possessions. Respecting someone's property means not taking or mistreating something that does not belong to you.

Why Are Property Rights Important?

Property rights belong to every citizen. They play an important role in equality. Property rights are important because they let citizens own their own property. They also protect people's property. Someone else cannot take it away or mistreat it. We can understand why someone would not want their possessions to be taken away or mistreated.

"Ultimately, property rights and personal rights are the same thing." —President Calvin Coolidge

Property rights also help protect important natural resources, such as water and trees. The government makes laws to protect water so it is clean and safe for citizens to use. The government also uses property rights to protect forests so that the trees cannot be cut down. Property rights also protect wildlife. The laws protect certain areas of land so that animals may live there safely.

Different Kinds of Property

There are different kinds of property. Some examples are **private property**, **common property**, and **public property**. Private property is something that belongs to a person. An example is a house or a toy. Common property belongs to everyone in a community. A local park is a kind of common property. Public property is property or land

Today, there are over one hundred thousand libraries in the United States.

CARNEGIE LIBRARIES

In 1895, a businessman named Andrew Carnegie (*left*) decided to donate some of his fortune to building public libraries around the world. He started by building libraries in Dunfermline, Scotland, and Pittsburgh, Pennsylvania. Later, he expanded to other parts of the world. By 1929, over two thousand libraries had been built. The Carnegie libraries offered citizens new chances to learn. Today, many of these libraries are still used. They are open to everyone.

Public libraries allow people to borrow and share books and other resources. They are a type of public property.

that is open to all citizens. Examples include public libraries, national parks, and lakes. Public libraries let citizens borrow books and use computers. National parks are protected by the government so that all citizens may visit and enjoy them. Lakes provide water for cooking, drinking, and bathing. It is important to respect public lands and public properties and not mistreat them.

Philosophers Plato and Aristotle discuss their ideas in this marble carving from the 1400s.

CHAPTER TWO

THE HISTORY OF PROPERTY RIGHTS

Property rights have existed for thousands of years. An example comes from ancient Greece, around 380 BCE. **Philosophers** Plato and Aristotle supported property rights. Plato thought that if citizens in a community shared the same property, there would be fewer disagreements. Aristotle disagreed with Plato. He thought that private property would be better for a community. He believed citizens would work harder to take care of property if it belonged to them alone and no one else. Plato and Aristotle's thoughts changed the way many people thought about property.

Influencing the Founding Fathers

In 1690 CE, an Englishman named John Locke shared his own ideas about property rights. Locke thought that the earth was common property because it belonged to all people. He also believed

 There are over 400 national parks, 560 national wildlife refuges, and nearly 250 million acres (101 million hectares) of other public lands in the United States.

a citizen could earn private property by working the land. For example, if a citizen worked a common property, like a field, until it grew fruit, the fruit would be the private property of that citizen. Locke

WHEN DO WE USE PROPERTY RIGHTS?

Property rights are used any time someone wants to build a home. A person first must buy the land or get the landowner's permission before building.

also believed that a citizen should not take too much private property. Instead, a person should share with those in need. Locke's ideas influenced Thomas Jefferson, the author of the Declaration of Independence and the third president of the United States, and many others.

Property Rights Today

The United States Constitution (*above*) was signed in 1787.

After the United States became independent in 1783, the country developed laws. These laws were written down in a document called the United States Constitution. In 1791, an idea called the Fifth Amendment was added to the Constitution. It protected people's rights in court as well as property rights. This amendment is still in place today.

"Property is surely a right of mankind as real as liberty."
—President John Adams

CHRONOLOGY

380s BCE Plato discusses property rights in his book *The Republic*.

350s BCE Aristotle talks about property rights in his book *Politics*.

1690 CE John Locke talks about property rights in *Two Treatises of Government*.

1787 The United States Constitution is signed.

1791 The Fifth Amendment is passed.

1833 The first tax-supported public library is started in Peterborough, New Hampshire.

1876 The first United States Supreme Court case of **eminent domain** occurs.

The Founding Fathers are pictured here signing the Declaration of Independence in 1776.

CHAPTER THREE

THE CONSTITUTION AND PROPERTY RIGHTS

The Declaration of Independence was signed on July 4, 1776. It said America was a new and separate country from England. This meant that American citizens no longer had to follow the laws of the king of England. The United States and England fought the American Revolution from 1775 to 1783.

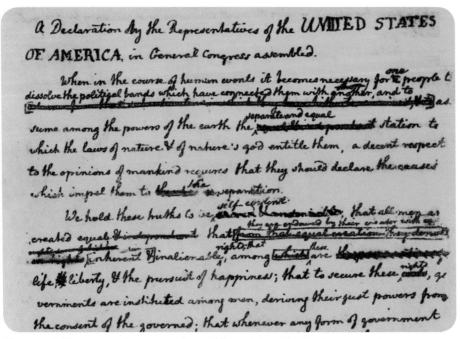

Thomas Jefferson made many edits while writing the Declaration of Independence, such as the ones pictured here.

The United States became a new country after it won in 1783.

Forming the Constitution

In this new country, a set of rules was needed. This set of rules was written down in the United States

Constitution. It was signed on September 17, 1787. The men who wrote the Constitution are often called the Founding Fathers. They helped to start the country of the United States. The Founding Fathers believed that property rights were very important. They made sure the Constitution included specific

Returning library books on time is part of respecting public property.

rights about property. Sometimes they did this with a change called an amendment. The first ten amendments to the Constitution are called the Bill of Rights.

The Bill of Rights are the first ten amendments, or changes, to the Constitution.

CARING FOR PUBLIC PROPERTY

Just because all citizens can enjoy public property doesn't mean all public property is free. Citizens must pay a fee to enter a national park or if they return a library book past its due date. These fees are used to keep parks clean and safe and to supply resources for libraries, such as new books and computers.

Each car must stop and pay a fee before entering a national park.

The Fifth Amendment

An important amendment to the Constitution was the Fifth Amendment. It was officially made part

It is the court's decision to take property away from citizens.

EMINENT DOMAIN AND THE SUPREME COURT

The first time the United States Supreme Court reviewed a case of eminent domain was in 1876. The case was called *Kohl v. United States*. The government felt that a private citizen's land would better serve the public as a post office. The court agreed.

of the Constitution in 1791. It states that American citizens have a right to life, liberty, and property. It also says the government can take away a citizen's private property. This is only done if it is for the good of the public and if the citizen is given something for the property in return. Taking property away is called eminent domain.

Keeping community properties clean is part of expressing civic values.

USES OF PROPERTY RIGHTS TODAY

Different things may come to mind when you think of property. Maybe you see buildings, land, your home, or your toys. Property is personal, and it is special to those who own it. It is important to remember that even if property is not your own, you should treat it with respect. Today, property rights continue to be important. They help your parents own a house, a car, or objects for your home. They also offer clean and safe places for

CIVIC VALUES TODAY

Many communities plan cleaning projects to keep their common and public properties tidy and enjoyable. Examples of those who practice civic values today are citizens who volunteers to clean up parks and beaches, or who collect food for those in need.

you to play, such as parks and beaches.

When you think of civic values, you may think of the Founding Fathers or the Constitution. You may not think they play a role in your life today. However, civic values and property rights are an important part of daily life, too. Whether

You can express civic values by respecting the property of your school and classmates.

Private property is another name for someone's home. It should always be treated with respect.

it is the school you attend every day or the home you live in, you live out civic values by respecting all of the different kinds of property around you.

"Buying a home has always been about more than buying a roof and four walls."
—President Barack Obama

GLOSSARY

civic values Citizens working together to benefit everyone in their community.

common property Something that belongs to everyone in a community.

eminent domain When the government decides that a citizen's private property is needed to better serve the public.

philosopher A person who studies many different points of view on many subjects.

private property A thing or place that belongs to an individual citizen.

public property Property or land that is open to all citizens of the United States.

FIND OUT MORE

Books

Harris, Michael C. *What Is the Declaration of Independence?*
New York: Penguin Random House, 2016.

Levy, Elizabeth. *If You Were There When They Signed the
Constitution.* New York: Scholastic, Inc., 2006.

Website

Kids.gov

https://kids.usa.gov

Video

Amending America: How Do We Amend?

https://www.youtube.com/watch?v=c_wbxHmSQKc

This short musical cartoon video discusses the process of
amending the Constitution.

INDEX

Page numbers in **boldface** are illustrations. Entries in **boldface** are glossary terms.

ABOUT THE AUTHOR

Kaitlin Scirri received her bachelor's of arts degree in writing from State University of New York College at Buffalo State. In addition to writing, she is also an editor with a special interest in children's books. Her favorite part of researching is learning about different parts of history.